old church was pulled down and a new one built, the new Saint Peter's Basilica. Another very famous man was hired to help in the work. He was Michelangelo Buonarroti—better known just as Michelangelo. He eventually painted the ceiling of the Sistine Chapel inside the Pope's house, and he designed the dome which today crowns Saint Peter's Basilica.

A Visit to the
VATICAN
for Young People

A Visit to the VATICAN
for Young People

**Text by Donald W. Wuerl
and Michael Wilson**

Illustrated by Piero Cipolat

ST. PAUL EDITIONS

NIHIL OBSTAT:
    Rev. Richard V. Lawlor, S.J.
    Censor Deputatus

IMPRIMATUR:
    + Humberto Cardinal Medeiros
    Archbishop of Boston

ISBN 0-8198-8002-7 cloth
ISBN 0-8198-8003-5 paper

Printed in the U.S.A. by the Daughters of St. Paul
50 St. Paul's Ave., Boston, MA 02130

The Daughters of St. Paul are an international congregation of religious
women serving the Church with the communications media.

Dedication
for Gianna, Denny and Donny

LIST OF ILLUSTRATIONS:

"An angel of the Lord appeared...and the angel said, 'I bring you good news of a great joy which will come to all the people; for to you is born this day in the city of David a Savior, who is Christ the Lord" (Lk. 2:10).

Nearly 2,000 years ago God sent His Son from heaven to become one of us—a human. Angels came to tell about the birth of the Son of God which was to take place in the town of Bethlehem. This small town is in the part of the world now called the Holy Land. Mary, a young Jewish maiden, was chosen by God to be the mother of His Son. Joseph, a good and just man, was His foster father. They called the baby **Jesus,** the name that an angel told Joseph to call the Child before He was born. Today we celebrate Jesus' birthday on December 25 and call that holiday Christmas.

Jesus was a very special baby boy because He was both like other boys but also the Son of God. He was the God-man.

Jesus grew up in another little town called Nazareth. When He reached a certain age, He began to tell others about His Father and the wonderful kingdom of God. To convince us that what He said was true He did all kinds of splendid things. He healed the sick, gave sight to the blind, helped those who were in need and even brought back to life a man who had died.

The name that the Jewish people in the Holy Land used for the great Savior-Leader they expected would come to make this world a better place in which to live was "Messiah" or "Christ." Thus Jesus was named the Christ—Jesus Christ.

When Jesus told us about Himself He often used figures and symbols. For example, He called Himself the Good Shepherd. He used this figure to tell us about His love for us. His love for us is so great that Jesus was ready even to die for us. Jesus told His followers: "I am the good shepherd; the good shepherd lays down his life for the sheep.... I am the good shepherd. I know my sheep and my sheep know me in the same way that the Father knows me and I know the Father; for these sheep I will give up my life."

In the countryside where sheep live it is the duty of the shepherd to watch over the sheep. He has to take care of them and lead them to fresh water and a place to eat. The shepherd also has to protect the sheep from wolves and other animals that would attack and kill the sheep.

Jesus said that He was the Good Shepherd who would not only lead His sheep to good food and fresh water but also defend them even if He had to die to do so.

Jesus also used the symbol of the good shepherd to teach us something else about His love for us. Even when we are bad, Jesus wants to help us. Even when we stray

14

Jesus told His followers: "I am the good shepherd; I know my own and my own know me" (Jn. 10:14).

away from His other friends, His flock of sheep as He called them, Jesus goes out to try to find us and lead us back. He told His followers that the good shepherd, if he has one hundred sheep and one of them wanders off, will go off to find the stray. "If he succeeds in finding it," He said, "believe me he is happier about this than about the ninety-nine that did not wander away" (Mt. 18:13).

Jesus is truly the Good Shepherd.

Jesus taught a message of love. He told us to love God and to love one another. He said: "You shall love the Lord your God with all your heart, and with all your soul, and with all your mind. This is the great and first commandment. And the second is like it, you shall love your neighbor as yourself. On these two commandments depend all the law and the prophets" (Mt. 22:37).

He also gave His disciples a prayer to use when they wanted to talk to the Father. One day while Jesus was praying in a certain place, "one of his disciples said to him, 'Lord, teach us to pray.' " It was then that Jesus taught them and us the prayer we call the Lord's Prayer or Our Father.

THE LORD'S PRAYER

"Our Father who art in heaven,
Hallowed be thy name.
Thy kingdom come,
Thy will be done,
　　On earth as it is in heaven.
Give us this day our daily bread;
And forgive us our trespasses,
　　As we forgive those who trespass against us;
And lead us not into temptation,
　　But deliver us from evil" (Mt. 6:9).

Jesus knew that one day He would go back to heaven to His Father. He had been sent down to earth by God the Father to make up for all the bad things (which we call "sins") which people did in the world and to try to lead us to a life of peace and love.

He knew that this could not be done by Himself alone in the short time He was to stay on earth. He knew that He must name someone to carry on His work when the day came for Him to die. So Jesus gathered around Himself many followers who were His disciples and a group of twelve friends who were His chosen pupils. These twelve were called the Apostles.

"The names of the twelve apostles are these: first Simon, who is called Peter, and Andrew his brother; James the son of Zebedee, and John his brother; Philip and Bartholomew; Thomas and Matthew the tax collector; James the son of Alphaeus, and Thaddaeus; Simon the Cananaean, and Judas Iscariot, who betrayed him."

(Mt. 10:2-4).

One day Jesus asked the Apostles: "Who do people say I am—a prophet?" Peter answered for everyone: "You are the Christ, the Son of the Living God!"

Jesus then said to Peter: "Blessed are you, ... I say to you, you are Peter (a Greek word that means rock) and on this rock I will build my church.... I will give to you the keys of the kingdom of heaven. Whatever you declare bound on earth shall be bound in heaven; whatever you declare loosed on earth shall be loosed in heaven." With these words Christ made Peter His very special helper.

17

"I will give you the keys
of the kingdom of heaven"
(Mt. 16:19).

The keys of the kingdom which Jesus gave to Peter are
the symbol or trademark of Peter as the leader of God's
Church. They show that Peter was given the power of Jesus
Christ to lead His followers. Today, when we see a picture
or statue of Saint Peter, he is holding a set of large keys—the
keys to the kingdom of heaven.

One night Jesus gathered His closest helpers—the
Apostles—and ate supper with them. He then gave them a
special remembrance of Himself. He gave them His own self

in the form of bread and wine. This special Bread and Wine we call the Eucharist or Communion. Today in Catholic churches throughout the world that Eucharist is celebrated in what we call the Mass. On Sundays and special holy days (or any other day) we go to church to share in Christ's Eucharist.

"This is my body... This is my blood..." (Mk. 14:22).
"I am the bread of life; he who comes to me shall not hunger..." (Jn. 6:35).

That same night Jesus was arrested by the people who did not believe Him. The next day the Roman soldiers who ruled the Holy Land killed Jesus. He was nailed to a cross and died. Jesus offered His death for us that we would stop doing evil things and do good toward God and our neighbors.

"Although he was a Son, he learned obedience through what he suffered; and being made perfect he became the source of eternal salvation to all who obey him..." (Heb. 5:8).

Since Jesus was the Son of God, death was not the end for Him. Three days later He rose from the dead. He came back to life, something only God can do. He appeared several times to His Apostles and other friends. Later He reminded them that He was going back to heaven and His Father. He also told them that they would have to continue His work on earth. "Go and tell everyone everything I have taught you," Jesus said.

"Go and make disciples of all nations, baptizing them in the name of the Father, and of the Son and of the Holy Spirit, teaching them to observe all that I have commanded you; and I am with you always to the end of time" (Mt. 28:29).

Before He returned to heaven, Jesus asked the leader of the Apostles, Peter: "Do you love me?"

"Lord, you know that I love you," Peter replied. Three times Jesus asked Peter to repeat that He loved His Lord. Then Jesus said to Peter: "Feed my sheep."

Again Christ appointed Peter as the leader of His Church and gave him the special duty of taking care of all His followers. Just as a shepherd takes care of and feeds his sheep, so Peter is to nourish and teach God's children.

The Apostles went to many different towns and villages all over the Holy Land and even farther away to tell people about Jesus. They preached to all the people they could find. They told them about Jesus and His wonderful resurrection from the dead.

Peter, who had the keys to God's kingdom, set out to find as many people as possible to tell about Jesus. Finally he reached Rome.

In those days Rome was the capital city of a vast empire that included most of the civilized world. It was a city with great palaces for the Emperor and the wealthy families that ran the empire. There were marble temples built to honor the various gods to whom the pagan peoples prayed. There was also a great chariot race track called the Circus of Nero where, later, Christians would be killed because they preached that Jesus is God and the Lord of all peoples.

When Peter arrived, there were no churches in Rome. The Christian community was still small and they gathered together in each other's homes to pray and celebrate the Eucharist. Peter found a family that believed in Christ and moved into their house. Fortunately, the Church was growing and there were several families that were able to offer Peter a place to stay.

Peter, like a noble captain of
God, brought the precious
word of spiritual light from
the East to those in the West,
preaching the good news...and
the kingdom of God.

23

Rome was the capital and center of a great empire. It was the city of the emperor or ruler of almost all the world.

24

Saint Priscilla, who lived in a large house on one of the fine roads of ancient Rome, invited Peter to stay with her family. The remains of this very old house are still visible in Rome on the street called the Via Salaria. Christian history tells us that Peter accepted this kind offer and remained as a guest in Priscilla's house during part of the time he lived in Rome and preached to the people about Jesus.

"Above all else hold unfailing your love for one another, for love covers a multitude of sins," St. Peter wrote to the Christians.

We can imagine Peter talking about Jesus to the many interested visitors who came to hear the wonderful story of the Lord from the lips of His number one follower. We can also imagine Peter leading the family and friends of Priscilla in prayer and the celebration of the Eucharist in memory of Jesus' death and resurrection.

From the First Letter of Peter: "Blessed be the God and Father of our Lord Jesus Christ! By his great mercy we have been born anew to a living hope through the resurrection of Jesus Christ from the dead...love one another earnestly from the heart. You have been born anew...through the living and abiding word of God" (1 Pt. 1:3, 22).

Not everyone, however, was happy to hear about Jesus. Many of the people who lived in Rome believed in the old pagan gods and did not want others to put their faith in Christ. One day these people arrested Peter and decided to put him to death. So Peter, the friend of Jesus, the leader of the Apostles, the first Pope, was killed. According to the accounts that have been passed on to our times Peter was crucified upside down because he considered himself unworthy to die in the same way Christ died.

Not far from where Peter was killed there was a cemetery on the side of a hill called the Vatican. This hill was just across the river Tiber from the center of the city and was a place where many poor people were buried. Peter was laid to rest in the hillside cemetery at the Vatican.

A very ancient writer of the history of the Church noted: "It is recorded that in the Emperor Nero's reign Peter was crucified and the record is confirmed by the fact that cemeteries there are still called by the names.... If you go as far as the Vatican you will find the monuments."

26

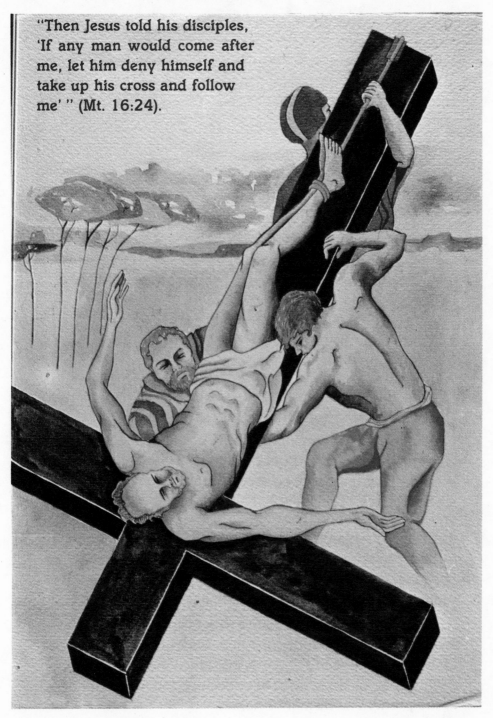

"Then Jesus told his disciples, 'If any man would come after me, let him deny himself and take up his cross and follow me' " (Mt. 16:24).

Now there was no one to run the Church in Rome and preach to the people about Jesus Christ. Someone had to be chosen to take Peter's place. Someone had to become the second Bishop of Rome. The earliest historians of the Church tell us that a holy man named Linus was chosen. He became the second Pope or spiritual Father of the Christians. The name Pope comes from the Latin word "papa" which means the same as we use it in English: "Father."

When Linus died another took his place so that there is always a Bishop of Rome, the Pope—someone to tell the Church and the world about Jesus. Since the time of Peter down to our own day there have been 264 men who followed in the position as Bishop of Rome.

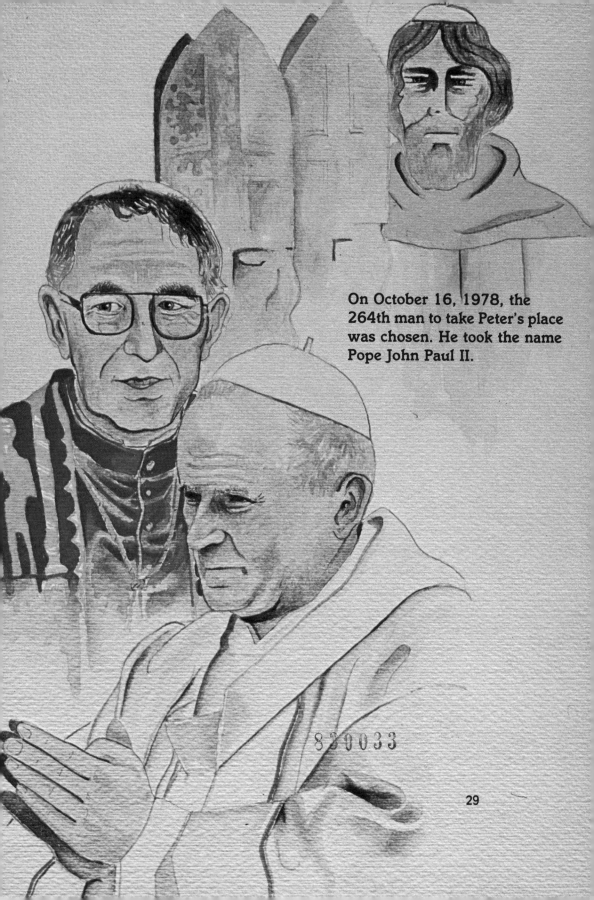

On October 16, 1978, the
264th man to take Peter's place
was chosen. He took the name
Pope John Paul II.

820033

29

For many years the Church had to suffer at the hands of those who did not believe in Christ. The Pope had to live in different houses and sometimes with different families because he did not have his own home as Pope. But all this changed in the year 315 A.D. when the Emperor Constantine became a Christian.

Constantine was a great general and fought many wars. He finally defeated all his rivals for the throne as Emperor of Rome. Once he was Emperor, he gave the Christians freedom to practice their faith in Jesus. The followers of Christ then began to preach publicly and to build churches.

By the time Constantine became Emperor there were many, many Christians. In every part of the world, from England to Arabia, from Germany to Africa there were large communities of people who prayed to Jesus as the Lord. But all these people looked on Rome as their center because Peter, the chief Apostle, had come to Rome. So Constantine decided to build several very large Christian churches in Rome.

The first great church that Constantine built was named in honor of our Savior. Later this church came to be called the Basilica of Saint John in Lateran. Next door to it was built a house for the Bishop of Rome. Saint John's Basilica was the church where the Pope taught and said Mass. Here the Pope placed the chair in which he sat while telling the faithful about the Lord. In Latin the word for chair is "cathedra." Thus the church where the bishop puts his chair from which he teaches is called a cathedral. The Church of Saint John became the cathedral of Rome. For centuries—over one thousand years—Saint John in Lateran remained the home of the Pope.

Constantine was the first Roman Emperor to believe in Jesus and become a Christian.

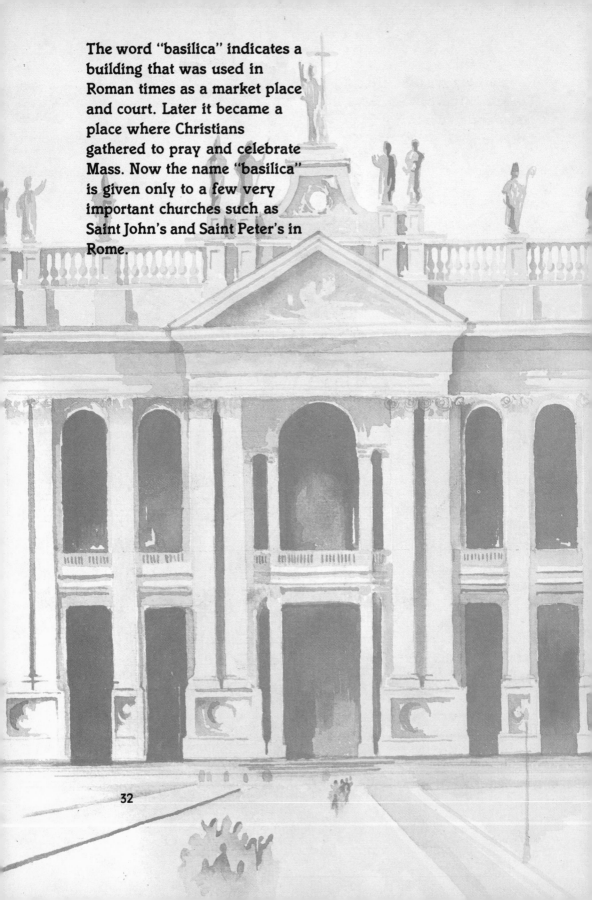

The word "basilica" indicates a building that was used in Roman times as a market place and court. Later it became a place where Christians gathered to pray and celebrate Mass. Now the name "basilica" is given only to a few very important churches such as Saint John's and Saint Peter's in Rome.

On the other side of the city, however, another great church was built by the Emperor Constantine. Over the place where Saint Peter was buried, a fine, large church was constructed. This church was built on top of the old cemetery where the body of Peter rested. The church covered the cemetery and the lower slopes of the hill that is called the Vatican. And so the church built on this spot was named the Basilica of Saint Peter at the Vatican.

Next door to Saint Peter's another house was built for the Pope so that he could sometimes stay at the Vatican to pray near the tomb of Saint Peter and teach the people in the great church of the first Apostle. Some people say that the first papal house at the Vatican goes back to the days of Pope Simmacus who reigned from 498 to 514.

As the years went by, the Pope's house at the Vatican grew larger. People from all lands and places came to visit the Pope. They brought him gifts and presents. Soon, the Pope had to enlarge his home at the Vatican. It changed from the little house next door to Saint Peter's Church to the large building that we now call the Papal Residence.

34

Saint Peter's and the Vatican you see today, however, are less than 500 years old. Pope Julius the Second, who was the head of the Church from 1503 to 1513, decided that it was time to rebuild the Papal House. He began the work that led to the present-day buildings and churches of Vatican City. Pope Julius picked as his architect for the Vatican building project the most famous architect of that time. His name was Donato d'Agnolo Bramante. From that day on the Vatican buildings were enlarged and expanded. They were connected with covered porches and arcades. But the major work of Bramante was to plan the new Basilica of St. Peter to take the place of the 1200-year-old one which was beginning to fall down from old age.

In 1506 the old church was pulled down and the foundations laid for the new Saint Peter's Basilica. Another very famous man was hired to help in the work. He was Michelangelo Buonarroti—better known just as Michelangelo. He eventually painted the ceiling of the Sistine Chapel inside the Pope's house, and he designed the dome which today crowns Saint Peter's Basilica.

For the next 100 years the work of building Saint Peter's continued. It reached its completion with the porch called "portico" in Italian, designed by still another gifted architect, Carlo Maderno. The whole building was finally dedicated by Pope Urban VIII in 1626. In the meantime such masters as Raphael, Sangallo the Younger, Giacomo della Porta and Domenico Fontana also worked on design and construction of this magnificent church.

Today Saint Peter's Basilica is the largest Christian church in the world.

A church is a building where Christians gather to worship God. For Catholics the most important act of prayer to God is the remembrance of Christ's death and resurrection represented in the Mass or, as it is also called, the Liturgy. The priest offers the sacrifice of the Mass at the altar of every Catholic church. For this reason the central point in the Basilica of Saint Peter's is the main altar. It is directly under the mighty dome planned by Michelangelo. On this altar the Pope celebrates Mass.

The altar of white marble is covered by a high bronze roof-like structure called a "baldachino." This covering is held in place by four twisted bronze columns 90 feet tall. All this is the work of the famous artist Giovanni Lorenzo Bernini, who took the bronze from the roof of the Pantheon, a Roman temple to the pagan gods.

Under the altar, if we go down several levels, we will come to the place where historians and people who study old buildings tell us Peter is buried. For centuries Christian tradition has held that this is the spot of Peter's tomb. Some years ago while Pius the Twelfth was Pope, men began to dig under the main altar and under the basement floor of the basilica to find the remains of the tomb in the old Vatican cemetery where Peter was buried. They uncovered large parts of the old burial ground and found the spot where Peter had been finally put to rest. The main altar in the basilica is right over the place where Peter's bones were found in the original Vatican cemetery. Every year hundreds of thousands of pilgrims make their way to the Altar in Saint Peter's to pray on this holy ground. They confess their faith in Christ and His Church which has Peter as its head. And the altar takes its name from the public act of faith and is called the "confessional" altar.

At the far end of the basilica, which is called the "apse," we find the Altar of the Chair, the second most important altar in this church. It takes its name from the large throne-like chair that hangs just behind and over it.

This chair reminds everyone of the Pope's most important work—to teach others about Jesus. This huge black and gold bronze chair, much too large to be used, shows how the Pope teaches when seated in front of this altar.

"Declare these things, exhort and reprove with all authority.
Let no one disregard you" (Tit. 2:15).

Artist Bernini wanted to make the Pope's teaching role even clearer, so around the throne he placed the statues of four of the greatest teachers of the Church, called the Fathers. Since the Church was begun by the Apostles both in the West (Rome) and in the East (Antioch) the statues of teachers St. Augustine and St. Ambrose show the Church in Rome and those of St. Athanasius and St. John Chrysostom, the Church of the East.

These four men, like many other famous men and women, many of whose tombs and statues are in churches all over the world, told the people about Jesus and His Church and wrote many books to explain the life and importance of Jesus.

Over the altar of the chair is a large window made of colored glass which shows the Holy Spirit of God in the form of a dove. When God wanted to tell us that Jesus was His Son, He sent His Spirit who came down from heaven and in the form of a dove flew over Jesus while a voice from heaven said: "This is my beloved Son." Today Christians use the dove as an outward sign of the Holy Spirit, God who comes to help us love Him and learn about Him.

The dove over the altar of the chair shows us that the Holy Spirit is with God's Church and helps the Pope to teach us correctly when he tells us about Jesus. When our Holy Father teaches us he is guided by the Holy Spirit. His words tell us the truth about Jesus.

"The Holy Spirit, whom the Father will send in my name, he will teach you all things and bring to your remembrance all that I have said to you" (Jn. 14:26).

If you were to walk from the Altar of the chair to the front door of Saint Peter's it would be like walking more than the length of two football fields. Each football field is 300 feet or 100 yards. The Basilica of Saint Peter is well over 600 feet long.

It is the largest church in the world. The dome rises 404 feet from the ground. All along the inside of this glorious edifice are chapels and monuments to Saints and Popes who have well served Christ and His Church. There are so many of these that it would be impossible here to talk about them all. But when you visit Saint Peter's you should not miss the black bronze statue of Saint Peter against a pillar on the right facing the Altar of the Confession. It has been venerated through so many centuries that the toes of one foot have been worn smooth by millions and millions of kisses. The baptismal font on the right as you leave the basilica is said to have once held the burial ashes of Emperor Otto the Second who died in 983 and was buried beneath the old Saint Peter's Basilica. The large dark red piece of marble in the center of the floor at the main entrance marks the place where, in the original basilica, the French king, Charles the Great, also called Charlemagne, was crowned head of the new Holy Roman Empire by the Pope in the year 800. Perhaps the most famous of all the chapels here is the last one on the left as we leave the basilica, opposite the baptismal font.

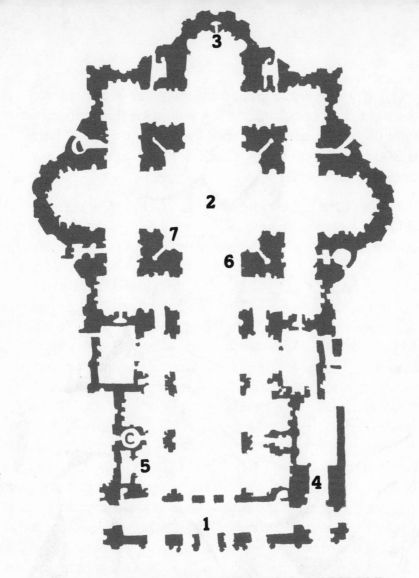

FLOOR PLAN OF ST. PETER'S BASILICA

1. Entrance also called "Facade" or Face of the Basilica
2. Main altar directly under the Dome and the Baldachino
3. The Altar of the Chair and Window of the Holy Spirit
4. The statue by Michelangelo, the Pietá
5. The baptismal font
6. The statue of Saint Peter
7. The entrance to the underground chapels and altar
   of Saint Peter

And Jesus was taken down from the cross and placed in the arms of His Mother.

Here we find the wonderful marble statue of Mary, the Mother of Jesus, holding the body of her dead Son after He was taken down from the cross. This statue is the work of Michelangelo who completed it when he was only 24 years old. The beautiful white marble tells us of the sorrow and pity of Mary, as she held our Savior in her arms after He had offered up His life on the cross for all men and women. The name comes from the Italian word for pity, "pietá."

Jesus died to save all men and women. He offered His life to His Father for us. His death was a wonderful thing for us. It freed us from sin. But it was also a very sad event. The statue, the "pietá," shows us the sorrow of Jesus' Mother, Mary, and our own sadness at Jesus' death.

As we leave the main door of the Basilica we enter the huge square called a "piazza," directly in front of Saint Peter's. On our left we can see the Pope's house. It is sometimes called the Apostolic Palace or Pontifical House. The Pope, our Holy Father, lives there. But this big building also houses and serves as offices for the large staff of helpers who work with him in leading the Church throughout the whole world.

The Pope is the Bishop of Rome but he is also the Bishop of the Universal Church, that is to say, the Catholic Church all over the world. He is the supreme or chief pastor of this Church. His diocese or "see" as it is called is important to the whole Church because the Pope, the Bishop of Rome, takes the place of Peter. The Pope is for the Church today what Saint Peter was for the Church at the beginning. He is the leader of the bishops and the spiritual father of all the followers of Christ. For this reason Rome is also called the Apostolic or Holy See or Diocese of Saint Peter.

The Catholic Church is divided into many local churches, each one of which is in the care of a bishop. A bish-

45

op is the spiritual father of all the Catholics who live within a certain area which is called a diocese. The Pope is the head of bishops and he keeps in touch with them as they carry on their work throughout the world. Every once in a while he can call them all to Rome for a meeting with himself. Or he can have them meet somewhere else and join them for the meeting. This meeting is called an ecumenical (general) council. At this meeting, over which the Pope presides, important questions and matters about the life and needs of the whole Church are discussed. The most recent of these meetings was held in Saint Peter's Basilica from 1962 to 1965. It was held at the Vatican, and thus is called the Vatican Council. Since it was the second such gathering of bishops from all over the world to meet in Saint Peter's, it is called the Second Vatican Council.

The responsibility for guiding so large a Church rests with the bishops and the Pope working together. But the bishops cannot all stay in Rome to help the Pope. They have their own local churches to look after. And they each have help in their own towns and cities. So, too, the Pope needs his own help to carry on his work as leader of so big a worldwide Church. With him in his house at the Vatican live many priests who work with him. These priests come from many countries since Catholics live in every part of the world. Together with sisters and other men and women, the priests all help the Pope answer his mail and give advice and aid to the bishops and Catholic people who live in the rest of the world.

All together there are about 3,000 helpers in the Vatican. This includes the highest ranking officials, called Cardinals. Cardinals are the special assistants or helpers of the Pope. Each Pope appoints certain bishops as Cardinals and then turns to them when he needs advice and help. These men wear bright red robes—the color of blood—as a sign that they must be ready to shed their blood for the Church. Not many Cardinals live in Rome. Most live in the cities where they are the bishop. But some stay with the Pope in Rome and take charge of his offices and act as his most important helpers.

Working with the Pope are many other helpers. These include doctors, bakers, telephone operators and even firemen. There are the people who type letters and take care of the altars in the basilica. There are priests who translate the Pope's words into many other languages so that every one can understand him, and there are people who keep the streets clean and the grass cut. Not all the people who work in the Vatican actually live there. Many live with their families in Rome. Only about 700 people have homes inside the Vatican.

The building we call the Pope's house is really his office building. Only a small part of it is used by the Holy Father for his own rooms. On the top floor of the building is the Pope's private apartment: his study, library, living room, dining room, bedroom and chapel. It is at the window of this floor that the Holy Father appears each Sunday at noon to speak to the people who come to Saint Peter's Square below.

The building as we see it today goes back to the time of Pope Sixtus the Fifth. He was Pope from 1585 to 1590. This Pope was a great builder and is responsible for much of the construction that went on in Rome to make it a more beautiful city.

The Pope's house is also used as a museum and picture gallery. Over the years, the Popes acquired works of art and received gifts from kings, princes, presidents and many other people who love him. All these gifts are now in the part of the Pope's house that is open for everyone to visit.

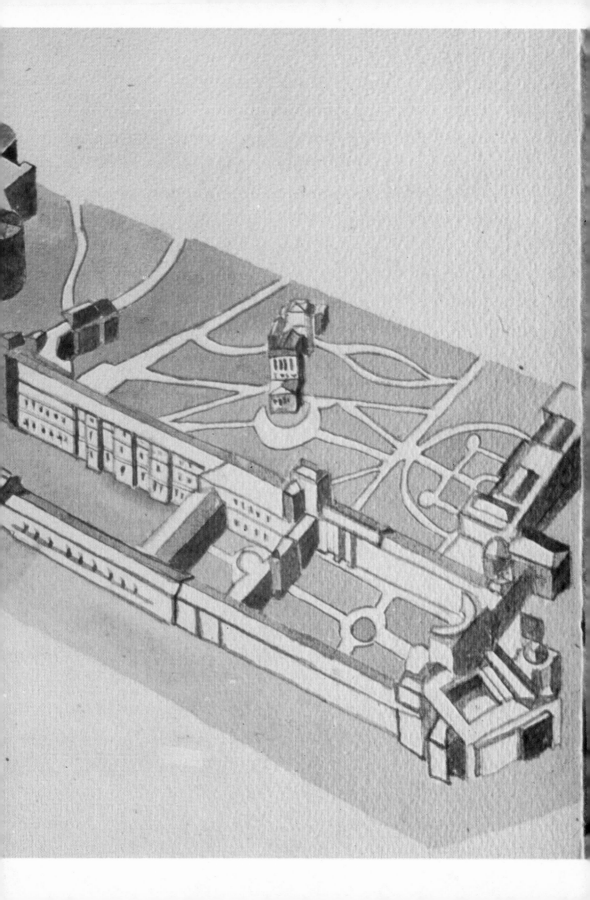

Prayer for the Pope

Father of Providence,
look with love on our Pope,
Your appointed Successor
to Saint Peter,
on whom You built Your Church.
May he be the visible center
and foundation of our unity
in faith and love. Amen.

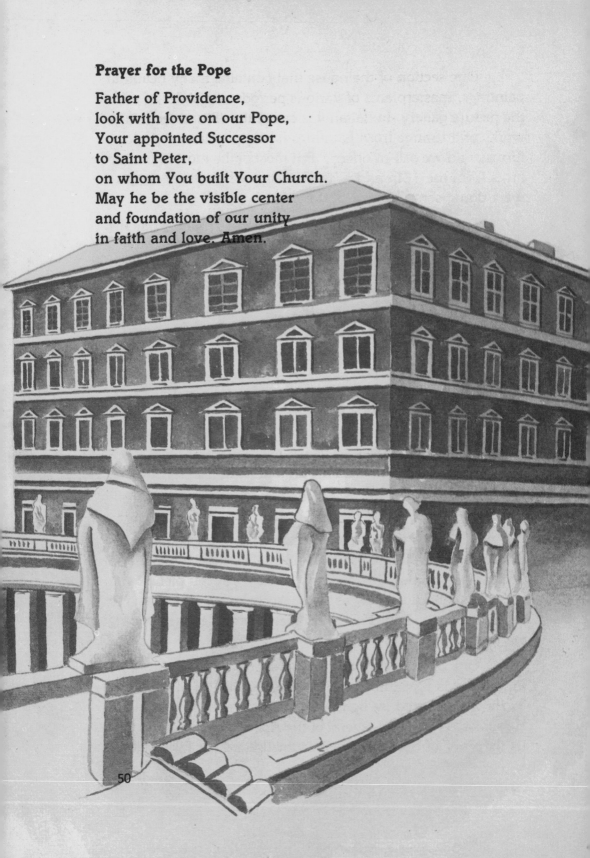

50

One section of the house that contains many beautiful paintings, masterpieces of various periods and styles of art is the picture gallery. In Italian it is called the "Pinacoteca." The works of art range from paintings in the primitive style to forms of art we call "modern." But most of the most important art is from the 16th and 17th centuries when Italian artists were doing some of their best painting.

The Pope keeps this collection of art so that now all the people who come to Rome can enjoy it. He acts as the protector of this wonderful art so that it is always there and available for everyone.

There have been collections of important ancient objects at the Vatican for centuries. But it was really only about 150 years ago that the Vatican museums as we recognize them today came into existence. In the early part of the 19th century (around 1805-1814) a series of wars was fought in Italy and the French Emperor Napoleon carried off much of the art and valuable paintings from Italy. In 1814 Napoleon was defeated and in the next year a meeting was held in Vienna to decide what to do with the art that he had taken from the churches of Italy. It was decided at this Congress of Vienna to give the things back to the Pope.

Pope Pius the Seventh gathered all this material and placed a lot of it in the part of the Papal House known as the Borgia apartments. This became the first Vatican picture gallery. The collection grew as more works of art were given to the Pope, and so Pope Pius the Eleventh provided the building we have today.

One of the many classical masterpieces found in the Pinacoteca is a painting by the artist Raphael. It shows Jesus as He was covered by light from His heavenly Father when He spoke to Peter and several of the Apostles. The picture tells us the story of how Jesus was "transfigured" or filled with

"Jesus took with him Peter and
James and John his brother and
led them up a high mountain
apart. And he was transfigured
before them, and his face shone
like the sun, and his garments
became white as light"
(Mt. 17:1-3).

light from heaven before the very eyes of His astonished disciples. This took place because God wanted to help the Apostles understand that Jesus was really His own Son. Raphael entitled this painting "The Transfiguration."

A museum is a place where things from past centuries are kept so that we can see what other people who lived long before us did. It is like an attic or cellar in our grandparents' house that is filled with wonderful old things that give us a glimpse of their lives and younger days. A museum is a houseful of exciting things from the days of the grandparents of the whole human race.

The present Vatican museum building also goes back to the days of Napoleon and the Congress of Vienna in 1815. This museum contains pieces of sculpture in stone and marble and all kinds of artwork from the days before the birth of Christ. For example, there are beautiful vases from the time of the Etruscans—the people who ruled the region around Rome before the Romans came to power. In this same museum we find a collection of art from the land of Egypt—the ancient kingdom of northern Africa on the banks of the River Nile. This kingdom existed long before even the Etruscans. The museum contains many wonderful stone statues of the leaders and important people of long ago and far-away kingdoms.

Much of the collection in the original Vatican museum is from the days of the Greek and Roman civilizations—about two thousand years ago. The ancient Greeks were masters of sculpture. They carved out of stone and marble very life-like and beautiful statues. They believed in many different gods and goddesses and so devoted much of their talent and work to making beautiful statues of them. When the Romans captured Greece, they brought to Rome many of these wonderful pieces of sculpture to decorate their city.

The Pharaoh was the ruler of
ancient Egypt. He ruled at the
time that Moses led God's people
to freedom.

One of these marvelous statues is called the Laocoön. It is a large statue of a father and his children fighting several huge snakes. This statue was made on the island of Rhodes 2,000 years ago. It was eventually shipped to Rome but was lost when fires destroyed parts of the city. It was not found until 1506 when some workers began to dig around the ruins of an old Roman palace. The statue is so finely done that Michelangelo called it "the miracle of art."

Another of the treasures shown in the museum is the statue of a young man. The statue dates from 130 AD and is a copy of a Greek original in bronze said to be the work of a sculptor from Athens. Because of its grace and beauty the man is called Apollo, one of the Greek gods noted for his youthful handsomeness. The statue is named the Apollo Belvedere.

Pope John the Twenty-third built a museum to house the Christian, pagan, and missionary art that he transferred to the Vatican from the Lateran palace. The latest additions to the collection of museums are the museum of modern religious art and the historical museum, both opened by Pope Paul the Sixth in the past few years.

The modern art museum contains paintings, sculpture and vestments, as well as modern chalices given by artists to Popes John the Twenty-third and Paul the Sixth.

In the historical museum we can see the ancient carriages that belonged to Popes and important figures from history, as well as the flags, uniforms and arms of the old papal army and navy.

There are two large coaches that were once drawn by horses. These were designed for long journeys over bad roads and it is believed that these were used by Pope Pius the Ninth in 1849 when he fled from his enemies at Rome and went to Gaeta in Southern Italy. There is also a very old American car, a Graham-Paige, that was used by Pope Pius the Eleventh and also a German-made Mercedes used by Pope Pius the Twelfth on July 19, 1943, when he drove from Saint Peter's to the Church of Saint Lawrence to comfort some of the civilians injured in the wartime bombing of Rome.

In this same museum is an impressive collection of weapons from the days when the Papal States had an army. Here we can see things from old crossbows to various types of rifles; muzzle-loaders, flintlocks, airguns, and more modern early Remingtons. There are hunting guns from many years ago, two bronze models of sixteenth-century cannons and a fine collection of swords. A prize exhibit is a model of the papal navy's ship, the Immaculate Conception, which sailed outside the port of Civitavecchia (about sixty miles from Rome) in 1870 when the Pope lost control of the city of Rome. This boat was ready in case the Pope, Pius the Ninth, wanted to leave Italy.

If we walk along the great galleries and hallways that connect the museum and the Picture Gallery with the Pope's House, we come to the Vatican Library. A library is a house for books. This particular library is famous because it holds so many old books and handwritten scrolls and documents. It has some 350,000 volumes and more than 50,000 handwritten texts called manuscripts. These include papyri or Egyptian documents written on paper made from papyrus reeds, a kind of tall grass. Some of these were done as long ago as 2,000 years before Christ lived.

Before the invention of the printing press everything had to be written out by hand. For example, in Europe long before Columbus discovered America, priests called monks, who lived in a house next to a church, used to copy on paper or dried animal skin the writings of all the famous teachers and learned people who lived many years before them. Many times the paper was rolled up into what we call a scroll. Some of these scrolls were lost. Many, however, were protected by

the Church so that other people could some day read and
enjoy them. The Vatican Library has some of the best
preserved and oldest scrolls in all Europe.

The founder of the library was Pope Nicholas the Fifth
in 1450. But the present building was built by Pope Sixtus
the Fifth in 1588.

Along the walls of the central part of the library are paintings marking the 16 Councils of the Church that had taken place by that time. The 46 cabinets along the wall contain Latin and Greek manuscripts. On walnut tables a number of particularly important and valuable books are displayed under glass covers. Unfortunately, very little of the very ancient documents from the first two centuries of the life of the Church survive because the pagan Emperor Diocletian ordered all Christian writings destroyed during the days while he ruled the whole Roman Empire.

On display we can see, among other things, a richly ornamented prayerbook of King Mathias Corvius of Hungary and an ancient Russian Calendar. At one table are a display of Martin Luther's manuscripts; the book written against Luther by King Henry VIII of England; King Henry's love letters to Anne Boleyn, whom he later beheaded; the oldest copies of the works of Cicero and Virgil.

Unluckily, full records of the early centuries of the Popes are far from complete. There are huge gaps because of uprisings and wars and also because the Popes would take their archives or records with them on their travels. It wasn't until 1417 that Pope Martin the Fifth ordered all records unified in the Vatican.

Despite all this there do exist two letters written by Pope Saint Leo the Great in 461 and Pope Saint Gregory the Great in 596. There is a diploma of Emperor Otto the First going back to 962, written in gold on purple parchment; a volume of letters by Pope John the Eighth from between 872 and 882; the original register of the letters of Saint Gregory the Seventh, written between 1073 and 1085.

The Bible is the book that records God's words spoken to us. God's words are so important that everyone should want to read what is in the Bible. This is true also of all those people who lived before books were printed. So we find many

"All scripture is inspired by God and profitable for teaching, for reproof, for correction and for training in righteousness" (2 Tim. 3:16).

Ἐν ἀρχῇ ἦν ὁ λόγος, καὶ ὁ λόγος ἦν πρὸς τὸν θεόν, καὶ θεὸν ἦν ὁ λόγος.

copies of the Bible handwritten and painted with beautiful designs. Some of these have ended up in the Vatican Library and are very famous. The most important handwritten Bible in the Vatican Library is one written in Greek. It was done sometime in the early fourth century. It is one of the oldest complete texts of the Bible still in existence. It is called the Codex Vaticanus.

From the Vatican Library we can walk down a long hallway into the most famous chapel in the world—the Sistine Chapel. This was the private chapel of the Popes and the place where even today the solemn ceremonies of the Holy See take place. It is here that the Cardinals from around the world gather to elect a new Pope when one dies. The building takes its name from Pope Sixtus the Fourth (1473-84).

Pope Sixtus also gave his name to the famous choir that to this day sings at all important religious ceremonies in this chapel or Saint Peter's—the Sistine Choir.

From an artistic point of view the most important parts of the Sistine Chapel are the ceiling and the wall behind the altar. Both these areas were painted by Michelangelo.

The Pope asked Michelangelo to make the Sistine Chapel very beautiful. Michelangelo decided to tell the whole story of creation in wonderful colors so everyone could see it and know how good God is to us.

The ceiling tells the story of the creation. In the beginning God created heaven and earth. He made everything that is. The first book of the Bible, called the Book of Genesis, tells the story of God's making or creating everything. God started by making light and separating it from darkness. He called the light "day" and the darkness "night." He then created water and dry land. On the land He made all kinds of plants and things that grow; vegetables, grains and fruits. Then He filled the sky with stars, the moon and the sun. To fill the waters which we call the sea, God created all kinds of fish and swimming creatures. He also put on the earth every kind of animal.

Finally God created man and woman. The Bible tells us that God created man and woman in His image. "In the divine image he created him, male and female he created them." Then "God blessed them." He "looked at everything he had made, and he found it very good."

The paintings of Michelangelo are called "frescoes" because they are made by putting the paint on the plaster while it is still wet and fresh. They point out in vivid color how God created the light and darkness, the sun and the moon, the trees and plants and finally—Adam and Eve. The pictures go on to tell of man and woman's first sin against God and how they lost the beautiful place God had given them to live—the Garden of Eden. The frescoes continue the tale of man's life with the story of the great flood that God finally sent to punish those who would not obey His laws.

The whole back wall of this chapel is Michelangelo's vision of what it will be like when Christ returns at the end of time to judge all men and women and reward or punish us according to how well we have behaved in this life. He called this huge fresco The Last Judgment.

The Bible tells us that at the end of time Jesus Christ will return as the Lord of all. On that day He will come in His glory escorted by all the angels: "then he will take his seat on his throne of glory. All the nations will be assembled before him and he will separate men one from another as the shepherd separates sheep from goats. He will place the sheep on his right hand and the goats on his left. Then the King will say to those on his right hand, 'Come, you whom my Father has blessed, take for your heritage the kingdom prepared for you since the foundation of the world....' Next he will say to those on his left hand, 'Go away from me, with your curse upon you, to the eternal fire prepared for the devil and his angels' " (Mt. 25:31-45).

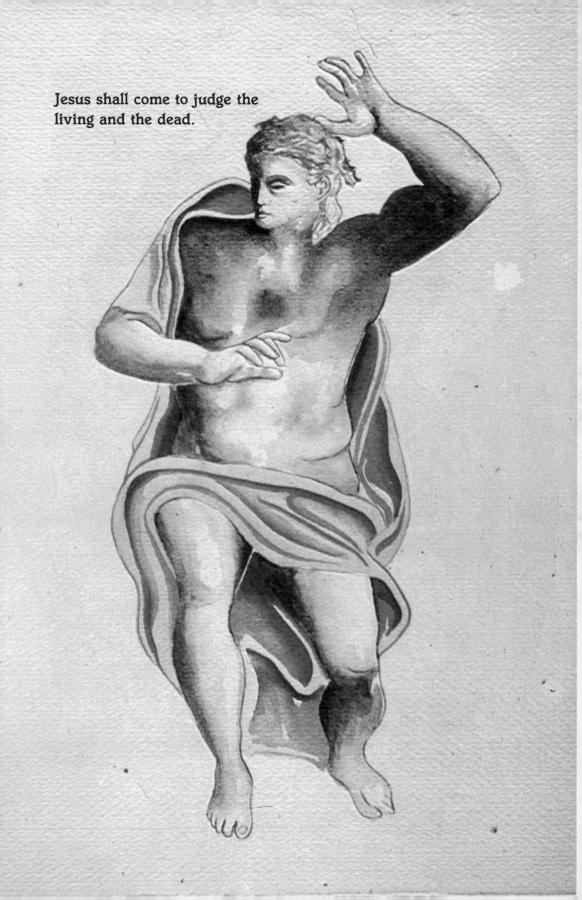

Jesus shall come to judge the
living and the dead.

Although some people visit the Vatican mainly to see its art works, most come also to see the Holy Father. For the Pope is the reason why the Vatican exists. It is his home. To make such a visit with the Pope more comfortable, Pope Paul the Sixth had the architect Pier Luigi Nervi design a large hall where meetings, called audiences, with the Pope could be held.

This building, the newest in Vatican City, is to the left of Saint Peter's Basilica. It is modern in design and can hold as many as 14,000 people. Every Wednesday the Pope holds what is called a Public Audience. At a set time he goes to this hall to visit and talk with those pilgrims and friends from all over the world who come to Rome to see and hear the Holy Father.

Although the Vatican has been the home of the Popes for centuries, in past times the Popes also ruled over a large part of Italy. In their efforts to establish the Christian faith and to bring peace to a troubled world they acted as a king and not just as head of the Church and father of the faithful. In today's world the Popes do not need, and do not want, any such large earthly kingdom. But they must be free to preach God's word, the kingdom of God, and to help men and women reach God. For this reason the Pope's house and office have been free from the control of any one king or president. The Pope is the head and leader of the land that he needs to keep the Church free. Once this land was rather large and was called the Papal States. Today it is a tiny nation inside the City of Rome, and is called the Vatican City State. It is only 108 acres or about the size of the grounds of the Capitol and White House in Washington, D.C.—tiny but big enough for its role as center of the Church.

Pope John Paul the Second gave
the name of Paul the Sixth to
the audience hall.

Although the Vatican is surrounded on all sides by
Rome, it is not part of Rome or the Republic of Italy. In 1929 a
treaty was signed between Italy and the Catholic Church. This
agreement recognized the Church's historic and very old right
to be free and independent in order to carry out its spiritual
mission of spreading the good news about Jesus. The treaty
set up what is called Vatican City State. Today nations all over
the world send ambassadors to the Pope at Vatican City. And

the Pope, in return, sends nuncios or delegates, all of them bishops, to these nations to help explain to world leaders, kings and presidents the Church's message of God.

Since it is an independent state, the Vatican must carry on the business that all nations do. Thus we find in the Vatican a post office which not only takes care of the Pope's mail but also prints its own stamps. These stamps are well known to stamp collectors who treasure them for their beauty. Every year since 1929, Vatican City has issued stamps. Many of the stamps commemorate religious holidays and events, but some show the Pope at his work or in travel. One of these sets of stamps shows the visit of Pope Paul VI to the United States in 1965 when he visited the United Nations in New York to pray for world peace. Another set shows the beginning of the pastoral service of our present Holy Father, John Paul II.

The Vatican State is one-third buildings; one-third squares and courtyards, and one-third gardens. Apart from the entrance to the museums there are several other ways into the Vatican. Perhaps the most famous of all these ways in is through the Bronze Doors designed by Bernini three centuries ago and which lead to the marble corridor and staircase that links Saint Peter's to the old Apostolic Palace and Saint Peter's Square.

"Take great care about what
you do and what you teach;
always do this, and in this way
you will save both yourself
and those who listen to you"
(1 Tim. 5:16).

Walk through Saint Ann's Gate into the Vatican and, to the right, you can hear the rattle of linotype machines and the whirr of printing presses. For the Vatican, despite its small size, has eight newspapers: an Italian language daily and two Italian language weeklies plus weeklies in five other languages—English, French, German, Spanish and Portuguese. The daily, **L'Osservatore Romano,** was founded in 1861 and all the papers have the same common purpose: that of reporting the words of the Pope, the papal appointments and the Church's views on events taking place all over the world.

There have been ten Popes since the paper was founded and its circulation has risen to 100,000 daily. Although the Holy See has been hemmed in by warring troops, such as during World War II, the newspaper fearlessly condemned Fascism, Nazism and Communism.

Separate from the newspaper plant, the Vatican operates a complete print shop which produces the many books and papal documents in all languages. This is known as the Polyglot Press.

The Vatican City State has a complete health service of doctors, a pharmacy and first aid stations scattered through Saint Peter's, the square outside and in the Vatican itself. This health service deals with Vatican employees, their dependents, and retired Vatican workmen. There are some 8,500 people who share in this medical service plan. These people are entitled to completely free medical, surgical and hospital care.

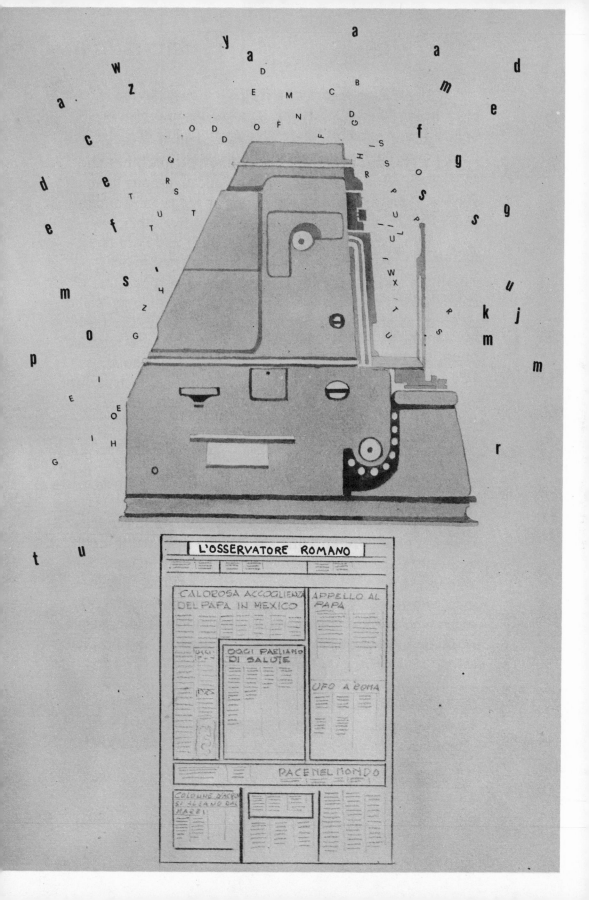

There is no record of a major fire ever having taken place in the Vatican. But with its treasures and historic buildings and contents, there is constant fear of fire. The state has its own fire-fighting service, with ladders and hoses capable of reaching to the topmost floors of the Apostolic Palace—and it can call on Rome's fire squads should a fire prove beyond its control.

One of the most used services of Vatican City is the railroad. Each morning and evening the double gates in the Vatican wall open to allow a train to enter or leave the Vatican to carry mail and food into the Pope's little nation. There is a railroad station but, since Popes today travel mainly by air or by car, the Vatican no longer has a papal rail coach. This is preserved in the Italian railroad museum.

Another important service of the Vatican is its radio
station. Vatican Radio is located in two buildings inside the
walls of Vatican City. There are also much larger studios outside the Vatican in other parts of Rome, and a giant transmis-
sion center some 20 miles outside the city. The first Vatican

radio station to be built was a brick building which housed the studio, microphones and transmitter equipment built by Guglielmo Marconi, the inventor of radio. In 1931 Pope Pius the Eleventh and Marconi opened the Vatican Radio which now broadcasts in more than 30 languages to all parts of the world. It makes it possible to listen to the Pope's words and other programs almost anywhere in the world.

There are two seminaries or colleges for Religious within the Vatican. The oldest of these is the Teutonic college. In 781 Pope Leo III gave Emperor Charlemagne a "piece of land by Saint Peter's" so that he could build a palace for himself and his successors. The only trace that remains of Charlemagne's palace is a marble plaque giving the name of the Church of Our Savior and stating that it was the duty of the priests who live there to care for pilgrims. Later a hospice, or guest-house, for German pilgrims developed on the grounds of what was the palace. Connected with this pilgrim center was a small cemetery for the burial of pilgrims who died while staying in Rome. It is the only cemetery in the Vatican. Today the building that occupies the land given to Charlemagne is the Teutonic college and it houses students from various parts of the world who are studying at one of Rome's many fine Church-run universities.

The other college is the Ethiopian College. The present building is new, opened in 1928 by Pope Pius the Eleventh. However, in the early days of the life of the Church, people from Ethiopia were constant visitors to Rome. The oldest still existing church in the Vatican was built by Pope Leo the First in 460 and set aside for the use of these pilgrims. The church was dedicated to St. Stephen of the Abyssinians— another name by which these people are known. Today only part of the church remains but we can still see the tombstone inscriptions of the Ethiopian priests buried here. Every First Friday of each month an Ethiopian College priest says Mass here for the Vatican workmen.

72

The largest building in the Vatican gardens is the
Governor's Palace. It is a sort of City Hall for the Vatican.
In it are the offices from which the Governor and his helpers
run the everyday work of Vatican City for the Pope.

Behind the basilica of Saint Peter and the Pope's
house we find the Vatican gardens (a kind of park) with
flowers and plants and paths through the grass and fountains.

The Vatican gardens are among the most beautiful in the world, very carefully laid out along the slopes of the 250 foot high Vatican hill. Almost every country of the world has sent samples of its native trees, bushes and flowers which have been planted in the gardens. Here the Pope can walk when he wants to get some fresh air.

In the gardens we find unusual and interesting fountains which add to the beauty of the landscape. Popes through the centuries have added to the collection of fountains and sometimes an animal found on the Pope's shield or coat-of-arms shows us which Pope built the fountain. There is a dragon over the fountain of the Sacrament and a large bird over the fountain of the eagle, both taken from the crests of Popes Julius the Third and Paul the Fifth. One of the most unusual fountains is that of the Galleon, which is a full-rigged lead ship with water pouring from the cannons.

Naturally, when these gardens were first planned, the chief gardener was a very important person and half-way, up the slope behind Saint Peter's is the house of the gardener. Now it is the headquarters of a group of men who study ancient buildings to understand something more about the people who lived many years ago.

You don't need a passport to enter the Vatican but at the main entrance, as well as in the doorways and passages leading to the Pope's rooms, you will meet the men who are directly in charge of protecting the Pope—the Swiss Guard. They still dress in the colorful yellow, red and blue striped uniforms said to have been designed by Michelangelo.

The Swiss Guard is the Pope's own small police force to help keep order in the Vatican. It also serves him on special ceremonial occasions. The Swiss Guard was first formed in 1506. Pope Julius II requested that 200 soldiers be sent to guard the Pope. These Swiss soldiers arrived in Rome in January of 1506. In those days many kings from

different lands used to fight to have a part of Italy. Sometimes these armies invaded Rome and even threatened the Pope. So it became necessary for the Pope to find some soldiers on his own who would protect him. These brave men take an oath—a solemn promise—not to let anyone harm the Holy Father. Some of the Swiss Guard have died defending the Pope. In 1527, 147 of the Guard were killed protecting the Pope during an attack on Rome.

Every year on May 6 this battle is recalled during the annual swearing-in of new recruits who take the oath of loyalty to the Pope with one hand grasping the battle-scarred Guard flag, thumb and two fingers of the other hand raised in the sign of the Holy Trinity, while the entire Guard parades in ancient armor breastplates, casques and drum and trumpet band.

The word Vatican brings to mind the Pope. It is his home. It is the place where he lives and works. When we visit the Vatican we are reminded of our special relationship to the Pope.

We call him our Holy Father. He is the spiritual father of everyone. Like our own father, the Pope cares for us, loves us and wants to help us grow. His special job is to help each one of us grow in love of God. For this reason he spends his time teaching us about Jesus Christ, the Son of God, and about God, our loving Father. He helps us by his prayers. He also works with the bishops and priests in every city and town to see that we receive the sacraments when we need them. In this way we can grow up not just physically but also spiritually.

When we stand in Saint Peter's Square in front of Saint Peter's Basilica and the Pope's house, we see the long rows of columns that reach out toward Rome and the world. They look like two long arms. They also remind us of the Church and the Holy Father who reach out to gather all men and women into one great spiritual family. This family is called the Church. Its leader in heaven is Jesus Christ. Its leader on earth is our Holy Father, the Pope.

Here in Saint Peter's Square people can walk in the sun on nice days and children can play without traffic to bother them. Here also on Sundays the Pope comes to lead his family of followers in prayer. He prays to God to be good to all of us—to bless us.

This is probably the most famous square in all the
world. It is nearly as big as all Vatican City. It takes its name
from the Basilica of Saint Peter. It is a large plaza closed
in on one side by the Basilica and on two sides by the long
rows of columns planned by Bernini. These 284 massive
columns and 88 pilasters (huge square pillars) are made of
travertine marble and together with the roof are called the
Colonnades of Saint Peter. They give the Basilica a long
curved porch on both sides. On top of this impressive set of
columns are 140 statues of saints from every age and land
who have shown their love for God and His Church.

78

In the center of the great square is a tall pointed column. This is called an "obelisk" and comes from Egypt. It was brought to Rome thousands of years ago by a Roman Emperor. Later when Pope Sixtus the Fifth began to rebuild Rome he wanted to place this monument in Saint Peter's Square. All his assistants began to plan how to move so big a stone pillar. They decided to put it into place by ropes. Once they got started pulling on the ropes the column got stuck. The ropes began to slip off the pillar. A sailor who was standing in the crowd yelled out "put some water on the ropes!" This the workmen did and the ropes stopped slipping and the column went into place in the square.

When we look at the obelisk in the square we are reminded today how each one of us can help in our own way to build up God's Church. Each one of us has special talents and gifts from God that we can use to help the Pope as he works to tell others about Jesus.

Every Sunday the Pope comes to the window of his house to see and talk to all the people who gather in the square. On very special occasions, like Christmas and Easter, he opens the big windows over the main doors of Saint Peter's Basilica and gives us his blessing. This prayer to God to help us is called the Holy Father's "Urbi et Orbi" blessing. It is his prayer for Rome and all the world.

The Pope's prayer asks God in the name of His Son, Jesus, and in the name of the Apostles Peter and Paul to bless everyone. All the people in the square then reply with their own prayer: "Long live the Pope!"

FOR FURTHER READING...

"You are the Future, You are My Hope"

Talks of John Paul II to young people of all ages. Reveals the stirring personal appeal of the Pope to the new generation. Excellent for youth and those involved in guidance. 326 pages, 16 pages of full-color photos.
paper $3.95 — EP1120

The Fisher Prince

Daughters of St. Paul
St. Peter, fisherman and apostle, the Rock of Christ's Church.
cloth $2.25 — EN0090

The Great Hero

Daughters of St. Paul
St. Paul the Apostle—adventures of the greatest among the pioneers and saints.
cloth $2.25 — EN0150

Footsteps of a Giant

Daughters of St. Paul
Charles Borromeo's tireless labor during the Council of Trent continued afterwards in fidelity to reform, to change of heart and conduct in the flock entrusted to him.
cloth $2.25 — EN0110

No Place for Defeat

Daughters of St. Paul

Pius V, the Pope who was a Dominican monk, renowned for his orthodoxy, his courage and mildness.
cloth $2.25 — EN0220

A Brief Catholic Dictionary For Young People

Daughters of St. Paul

This handy pamphlet-dictionary defines simply and clearly the words most often used in religious education today.
30 pages. 75¢ — CH0125

The Church's Amazing Story

This adventure-packed book presents the story of the Church from its foundation until today! Life-sketches of important persons—kings, bishops, missionaries, saints and martyrs—bring them to life and spark interest. This book reinforces the reader's conviction that the Catholic Church is truly Christ's own and He will be with it until the end of time as He promised.
cloth $4.00, paper $3.00 — CA0100T

Please order from any of the following addresses. Kindly specify title, item number and binding. Include 60¢ postage for one book and 15¢ for each additional book.

Daughters of St. Paul

IN MASSACHUSETTS
   50 St. Paul's Ave. Jamaica Plain, Boston, MA 02130;
      617-522-8911; 617-522-0875;
   172 Tremont Street, Boston, MA 02111; **617-426-5464;**
      617-426-4230
IN NEW YORK
   78 Fort Place, Staten Island, NY 10301; **212-447-5071**
   59 East 43rd Street, New York, NY 10017; **212-986-7580**
   7 State Street, New York, NY 10004; **212-447-5071**
   625 East 187th Street, Bronx, NY 10458; **212-584-0440**
   525 Main Street, Buffalo, NY 14203; **716-847-6044**
IN NEW JERSEY
   Hudson Mall — Route 440 and Communipaw Ave.,
      Jersey City, NJ 07304; **201-433-7740**
IN CONNECTICUT
   202 Fairfield Ave., Bridgeport, CT 06604; **203-335-9913**
IN OHIO
   2105 Ontario St. (at Prospect Ave.), Cleveland, OH 44115; **216-621-9427**
   25 E. Eighth Street, Cincinnati, OH 45202; **513-721-4838**
IN PENNSYLVANIA
   1719 Chestnut Street, Philadelphia, PA 19103; **215-568-2638**
IN FLORIDA
   2700 Biscayne Blvd., Miami, FL 33137; **305-573-1618**
IN LOUISIANA
   4403 Veterans Memorial Blvd., Metairie, LA 70002; **504-887-7631;**
      504-887-0113
   1800 South Acadian Thruway, P.O. Box 2028, Baton Rouge, LA 70821
      504-343-4057; 504-343-3814
IN MISSOURI
   1001 Pine Street (at North 10th), St. Louis, MO 63101; **314-621-0346;**
      314-231-1034
IN ILLINOIS
   172 North Michigan Ave., Chicago, IL 60601; **312-346-4228**
IN TEXAS
   114 Main Plaza, San Antonio, TX 78205; **512-224-8101**
IN CALIFORNIA
   1570 Fifth Avenue, San Diego, CA 92101; **714-232-1442**
   46 Geary Street, San Francisco, CA 94108; **415-781-5180**
IN HAWAII
   1143 Bishop Street, Honolulu, HI 96813; **808-521-2731**
IN ALASKA
   750 West 5th Avenue, Anchorage AK 99501; **907-272-8183**
IN CANADA
   3022 Dufferin Street, Toronto 395, Ontario, Canada
IN ENGLAND
   128, Notting Hill Gate, London W11 3QG, England
133 Corporation Street, Birmingham B4 6PH, England
5A-7 Royal Exchange Square, Glasgow G1 3AH, England
82 Bold Street, Liverpool L1 4HR, England
IN AUSTRALIA
   58 Abbotsford Rd., Homebush, N.S.W., Sydney 2140, Australia